THE DEEP DARK SEA

THE DEEP DARK SEA

Written and illustrated by
TONY DE SAULLES

Orion
Children's Books

First published in Great Britain in 2015
by Orion Children's Books
a division of the Orion Publishing Group Ltd
Orion House
5 Upper Saint Martin's Lane
London WC2H 9EA
An Hachette UK Company

1 3 5 7 9 10 8 6 4 2

The Orion Publishing Group's policy is to use papers that
are natural, renewable and recyclable products and made
from wood grown in sustainable forests. The logging and
manufacturing processes are expected to conform to the
environmental regulations of the country of origin.

ISBN 978 1 4440 1548 5

A catalogue record for this book is available
from the British Library.

Printed and bound in China

www.orionbooks.co.uk

*To Frank from Uncle Tony –
get reading!*

CONTENTS

1. How deep is the sea?   11

2. What is alive down there?   19

3. Incredible creatures   29

4. Hungry hunters   41

5. Finding food in the dark   51

6. How not to get eaten   63

1
How deep is the sea?

Our planet is green and blue.
Green land and blue sea.

There is a lot more sea than land.
If Earth was a big cake,
the green slice would only be this big.

Yuk! This cake tastes fishy!

Did you know that there are more creatures in the sea than there are on land?

The shore is where the land meets the sea.
When you paddle in the water you feel the
sand under your feet.

As you go **DEEPER** the water
gets darker and colder.

The sea is very VERY deep.
If you put Mount Everest (the highest
mountain in the world) at the bottom
of the deepest part of the sea and then
put the highest building in the world
on top of that you would still
have lots of water above you!

Let's dive down and explore
the deep dark sea.

2
What is alive down there?

Would you like to live somewhere cold
and dark with deadly pressure
and poisonous gases?

If you go too deep you will feel
the water squashing you.
This squashing feeling is called pressure.

The **deeper** you go the **harder** the water will press against you.

On land volcanoes spit out fire and gas.

It is the same in some of the deepest parts of the sea.

Cough!

A hundred and fifty years ago scientists thought that nothing could be alive in such a dangerous place. But then fishermen started to catch strange sea creatures.

Inventors made diving suits to explore
under water but the strong pressure
stopped them from going very deep.

This suit was used
300 years ago.

And this
one is from
150 years ago.

It is only in the last few years that scientists have been able to build machines to explore the deep sea.

A world of incredible creatures.

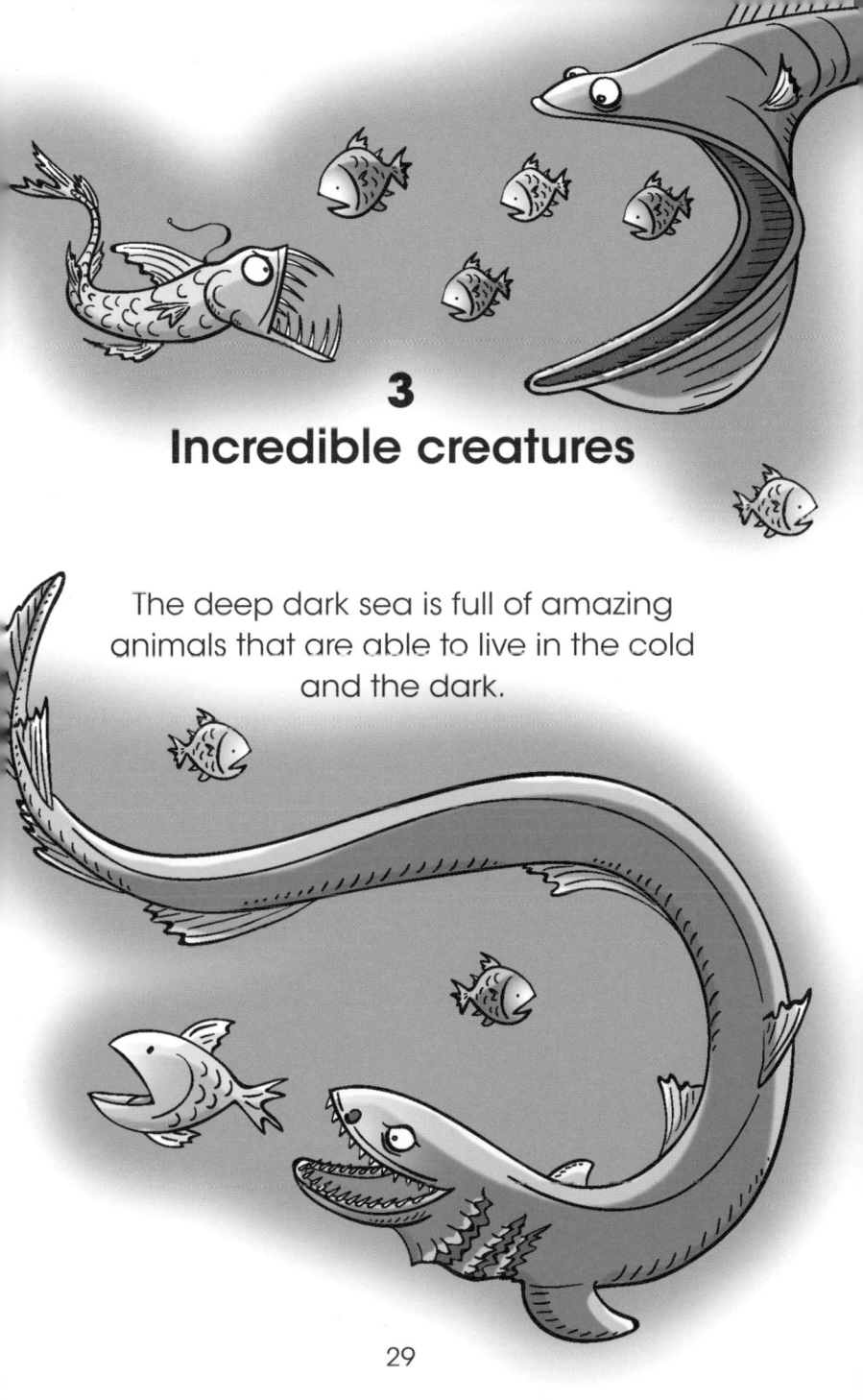

3
Incredible creatures

The deep dark sea is full of amazing animals that are able to live in the cold and the dark.

Giant isopods move across the sea floor.
They are relatives of the little woodlice
you find under rocks in the garden.

These strange creatures are called
bone-eating snot-flower worms.
They feed on the bones of dead whales
that have sunk to the bottom of the sea.

Do you use a sponge in the bath?

Beautiful **sponges** live in the deep sea.
They filter tiny bits of food from the water.

Scientists have even found deep-sea sponges that catch and eat small sea animals.

Octopus, and **jellyfish** suck water
into their bodies. Then they blast it out to
push themselves along.

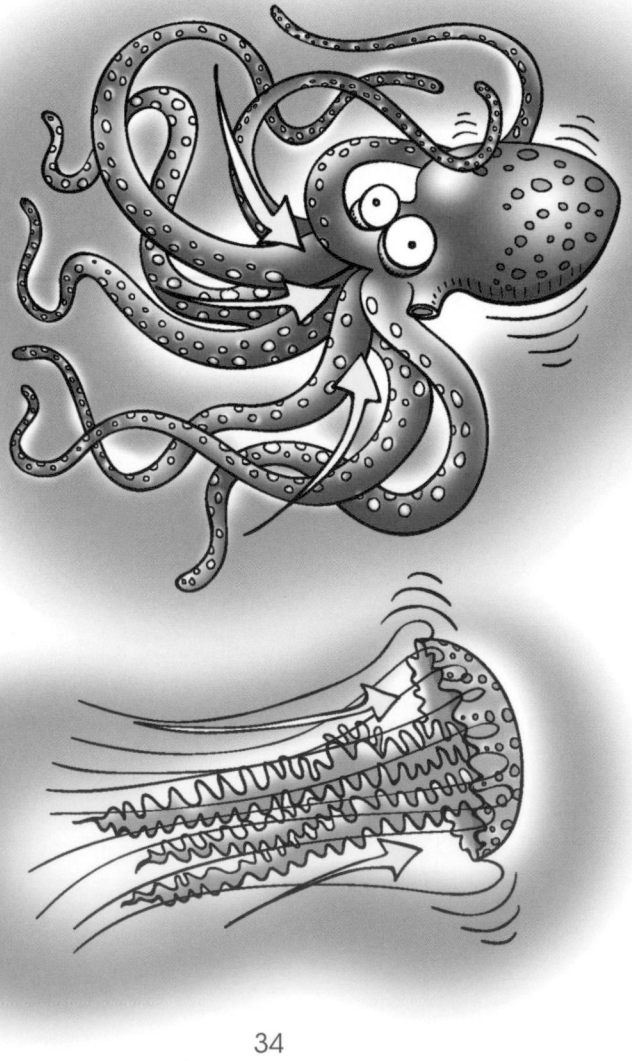

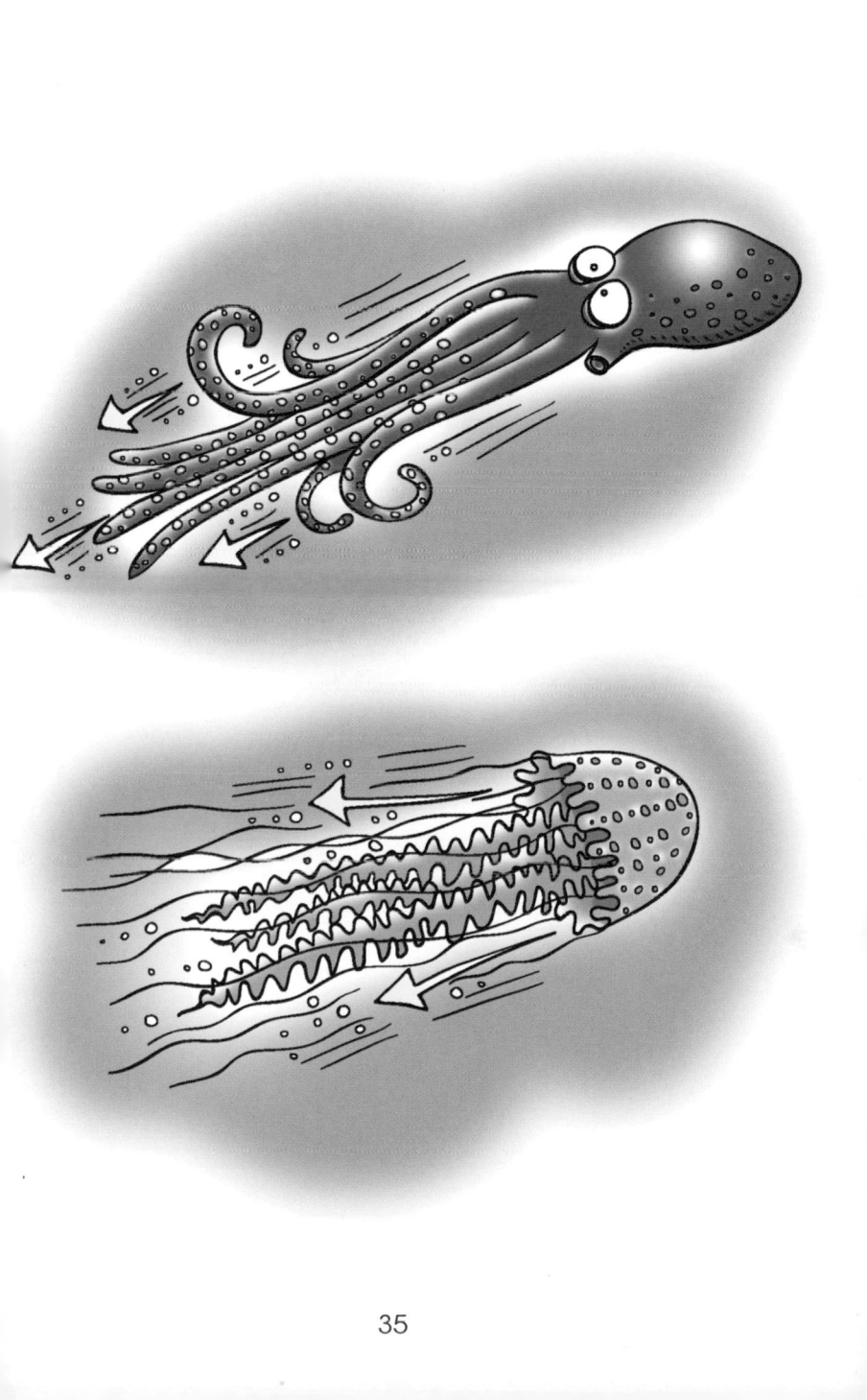

The **dumbo octopus** has a different way of moving through the water. It flaps its fins that look like the ears of Dumbo the elephant!

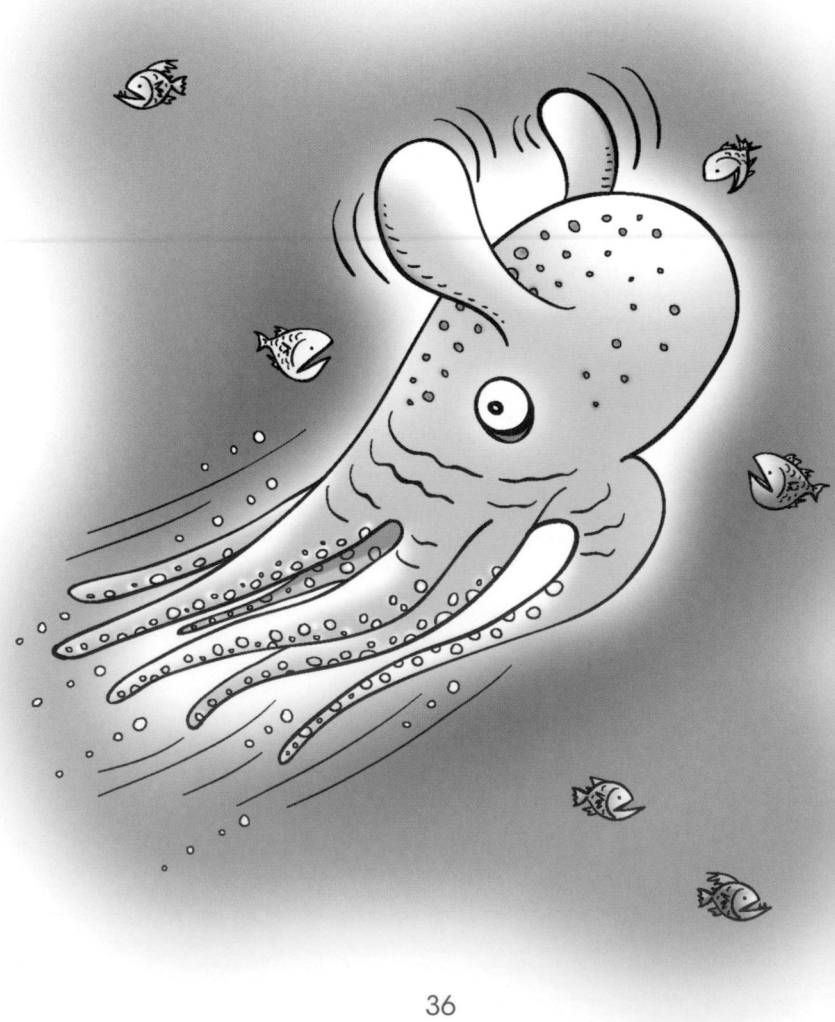

Lantern fish light up the water.
Their glow-in-the-dark bodies tell other
lantern fish that they are nearby.

The **lizardfish** waits to pounce on passing sea creatures. It has a mouth full of sharp fangs and even has teeth on its tongue!

The **viperfish** has such big teeth
that it can't close its mouth.
Can you imagine having teeth that big?

4
Hungry hunters

Bigger sea creatures also hunt for food.

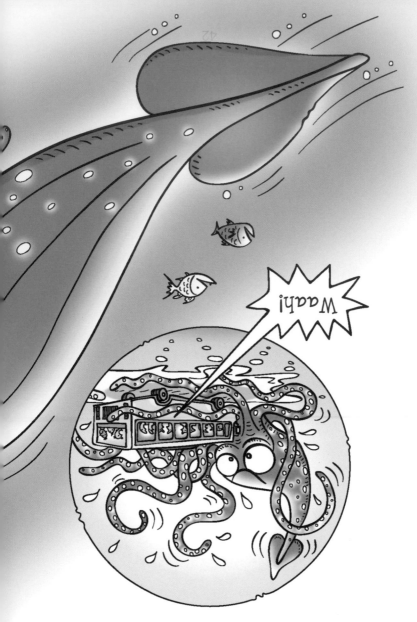

Giant squid can grow as long as a bus and have eyes as big as dinner plates.

They grab big fish
with their tentacles
and stuff them into
their mouths.

Hungry sharks glide through the water.

The **goblin shark** looks like an alien.
It has a sensitive nose for finding fish and a
frightening set of teeth for catching them.

He's goblin' me up!

The **megamouth shark** is harder to spot. It comes to the surface at night with its huge mouth wide open to catch jellyfish and tiny sea creatures called plankton.

80 million-year-old fossils of the **frill shark** tell us that these prehistoric creatures were swimming in the deep sea while dinosaurs roamed the land.

Aaah!

But frill sharks are
still alive today
slithering through
the dark depths
and feeding on
squid and fish.

There are even mammals like the
sperm whale and the **elephant seal**
that hunt for food in the deep sea.

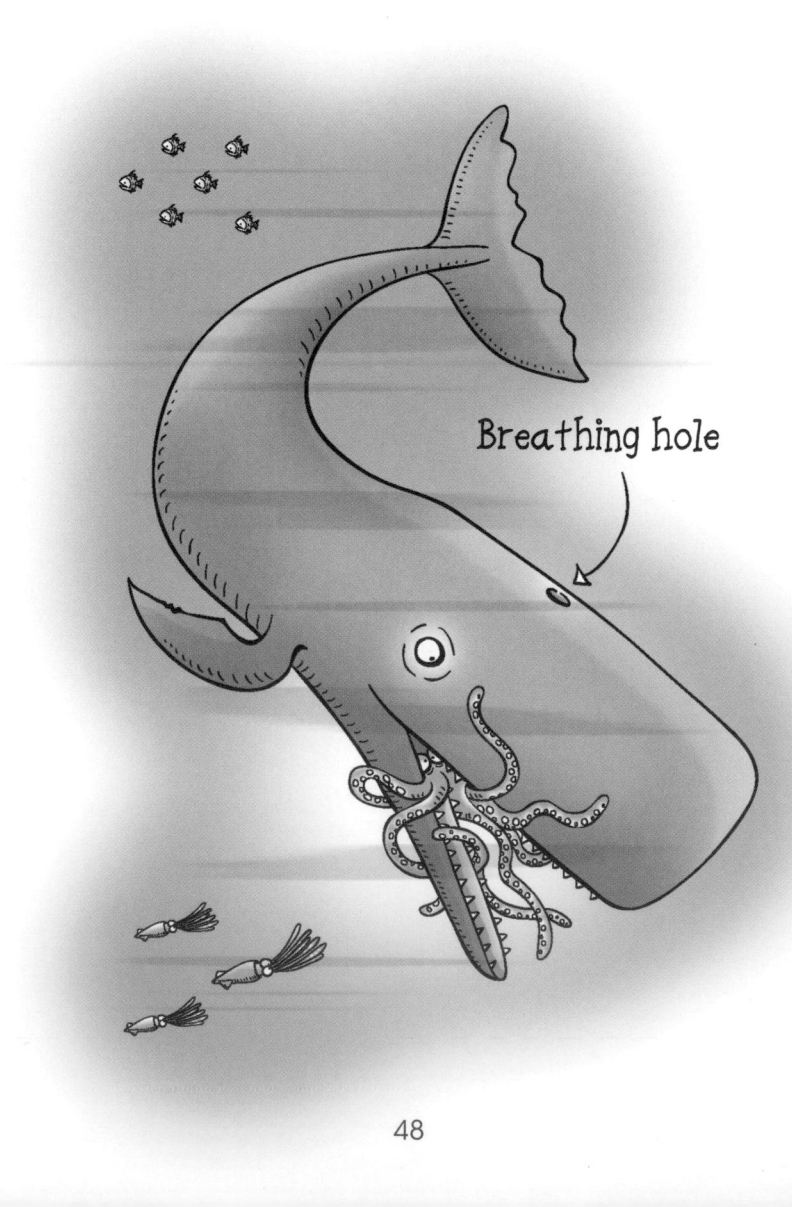

Breathing hole

Breathing holes

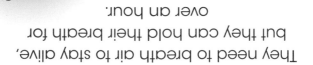

They need to breath air to stay alive,
but they can hold their breath for
over an hour.

You are a mammal too.
Can you hold your breath for ten seconds?

Breathing holes

5
Finding food in the dark

When fish and other sea animals die
they rot and sink to the seabed.

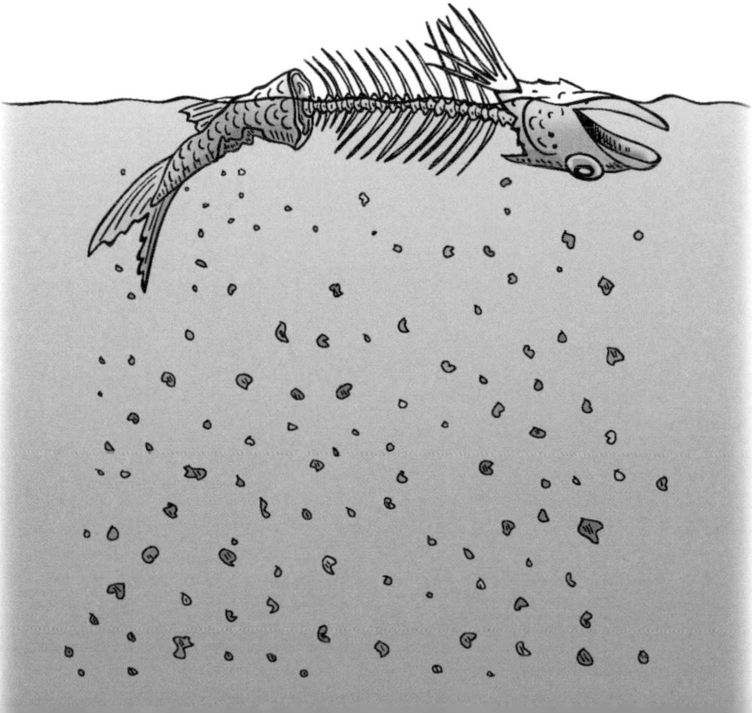

The rotting bits fall like snow and
feed the little fish below.
And little fish provide food for bigger fish.

But how do bigger fish find food
in the dark?

The **anglefish** dangles a glowing light
from its head.

Small fish swim close to the glow thinking
it might be food.

But the small fish end up as food
for the anglerfish.

The **snaggletooth** also has a glowing light to attract small fish. This light hangs from its chin!

But lunch is hard to find and like many other deep-sea animals, the snaggletooth sometimes goes for weeks without food.

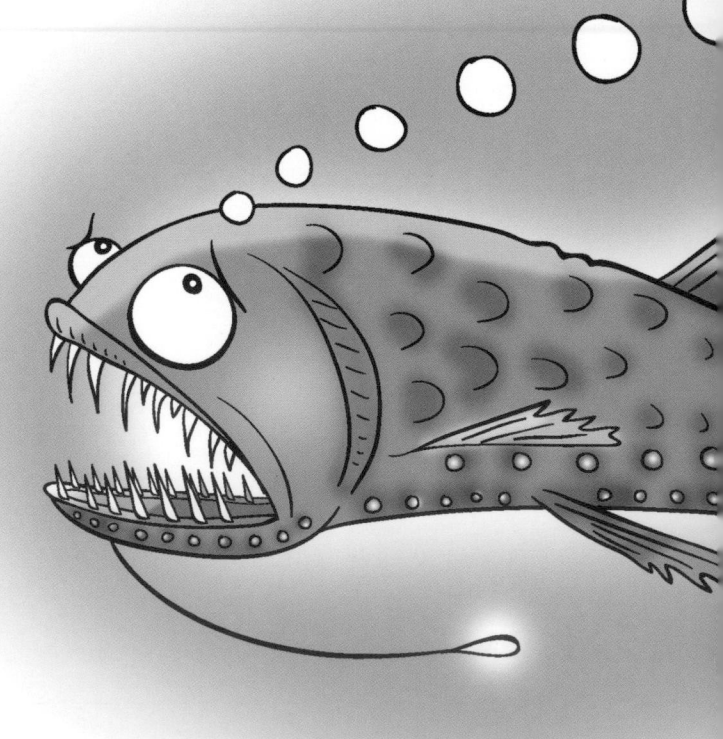

Most fish do not see the red beam
of the **stoplight loosejaw fish**.
This makes it invisible
so it can sneak up
to grab its dinner.

It has a massive
mouth for
catching fish.

Can you guess how the
rattail fish got its name? Of course!

It has a long thin body that
looks like a rat's tail. A long fin
runs under it that can feel tiny
movements in the water.
This helps it to find shrimp and
small squid in the dark.

Lots of deep-sea fish need big mouths
to catch food in the dark.
The **gulper eel** has a giant mouth
and can eat animals that are
bigger than it is.

You and your big mouth!

Some deep-sea fish have stomachs that can stretch to hold big fish that they have eaten.

This anglerfish hasn't had anything to eat for a while.

But look how much it has stretched
after catching a big fish!

6
How not to get eaten

The deep dark sea can be dangerous but many animals have clever ways to protect themselves.

Glowing **hatchet fish** blend with the lighter water above to hide from sharks and big fish.

They also have big eyes in the top of their head to help them spot danger from above.

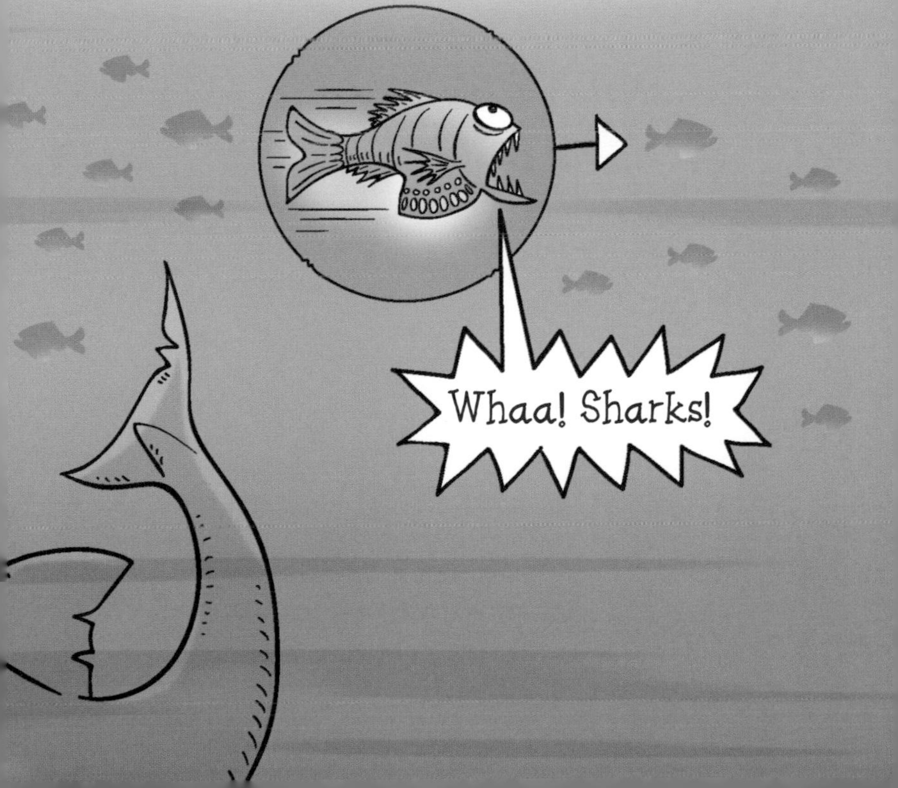

Whaa! Sharks!

Green bomber worms scare away attackers by releasing glowing green bombs from their heads!

Flashlight fish can switch their glowing eyes
on and off to confuse bigger fish.

The **vampire squid** turns itself inside out when attackers come near.

The bottom of the sea is an amazing world. But it is a dark and dangerous place too. Only a tiny part has been explored so far.

Scientists think there are lots more creatures waiting to be found but it will take a long time to discover all the secrets of the deep dark sea.

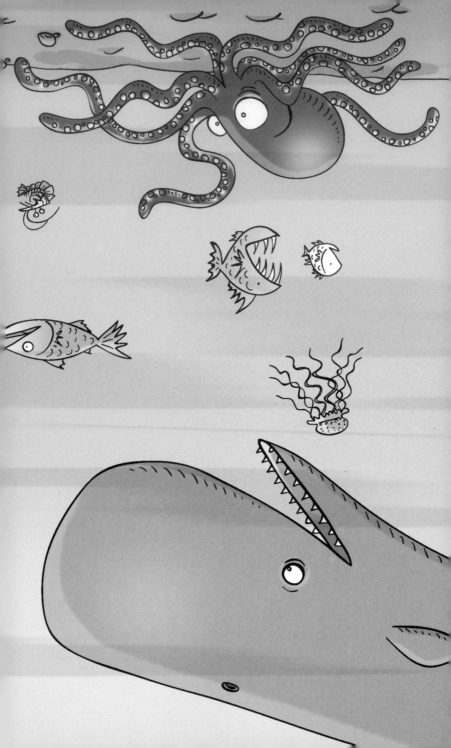

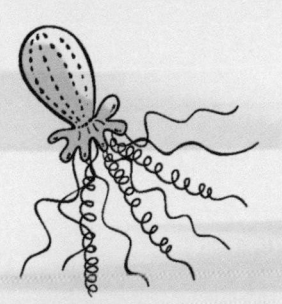

How much do you know?

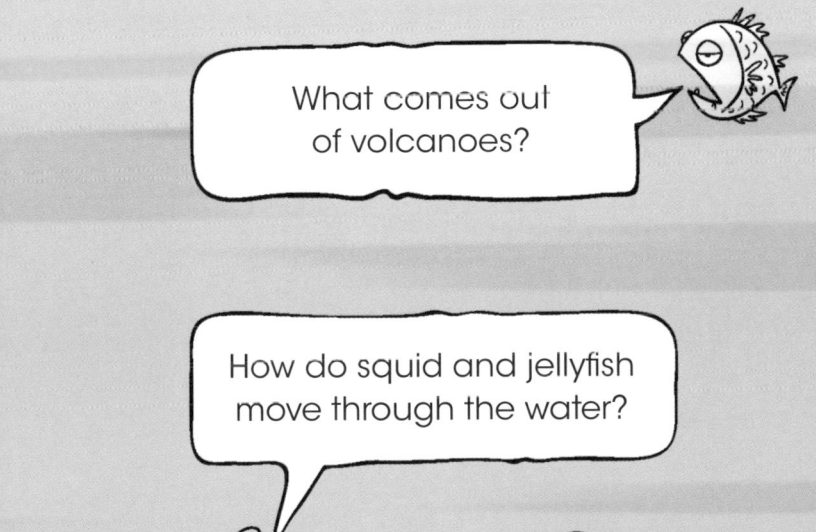

What comes out of volcanoes?

How do squid and jellyfish move through the water?

Dive into the
deep dark sea.

Come face to face
with incredible
dinosaurs.

DISCOVER NEXT?

Take a look at your own back garden.

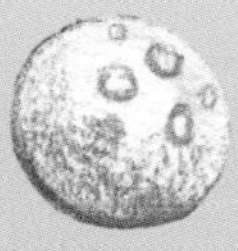

Speed off to outer space.

It's never too early to find out more.

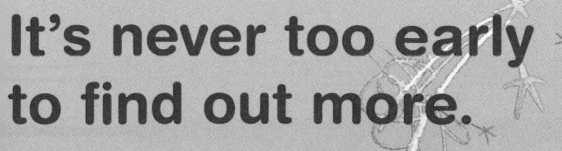